Donna

Thought you could do
with a few belated
hints!

much love,
Jennifer ♡
Louise.

A Wife's Guide to Pro Football

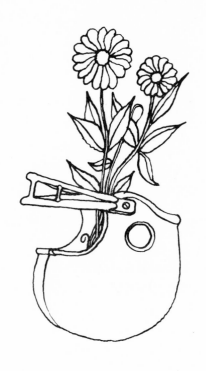

A Wife's Guide to Pro Football

by Elaine Tarkenton and Michael Rich

With unscrambled notes by Fran Tarkenton

NEW YORK / THE VIKING PRESS

To the long-suffering wives of pro football fans—with the hope that in some small way this book can explain and communicate the fascination of The Game for husbands everywhere.

First published in 1969 by The Viking Press, Inc.
625 Madison Avenue, New York, N.Y. 10022

Published simultaneously in Canada by
The Macmillan Company of Canada Limited

Library of Congress catalog card number: 77-83239

Printed in U.S.A.

Contents

Introduction

"Hut one. Hut two."

The call of the quarterback. Every fall, it summons 300,000 pro-football fans to a Sunday afternoon of edge-of-the-seat excitement at stadiums across the nation. While at home, some seventeen *million* American men draw close to their TV sets, absorbed in the suspense, the violence, the drama of what has become The Game: professional football.

And what are the wives of these enraptured fans doing?

A few, a very few, share the excitement of the game with their husbands. But for most, Sunday afternoon means hours of pro-football widowhood ——a slam-the-door retreat to kitchen or bedroom in an often unsuccessful attempt to get beyond range of a sportscaster whose excitement is reflected in a rising crescendo of incomprehensibility, from a tense "Third and inches, triple flankers right" to a shrieking "He breaks out into the clear."

Moreover, the amount of time a fan invests in his favorite sport—and away from you—is increasing. If your husband goes to the game he may leave the house on Sunday at 11:00 A.M., or earlier— to find a parking place, watch the pre-game drills, or have lunch with his friends. If he's watching it on television, he probably settles into a chair to watch the pre-game shows that generally begin an hour before the kickoff. And now that TV sometimes offers a pro-football doubleheader, with one game from the East being followed by another from the West, your marriage can be rendered hors de television for six hours or more.

The foregoing is probably why pro football is, for most wives, synonymous with the Sunday blahs. Worst of all, after you've resigned yourself to being ignored for most of the day—have patiently borne his imprecations hurled at plays gone wrong, his cheering at plays gone right—his team loses. More often than not, he will then fall prey to the "tragic-fan" syndrome—a disease whose symptoms include yelling at the kids for no reason, kicking the dog, and telling you that his mother's cooking is better than yours.

In a sense, then, this book is concerned with marital counseling. But mostly, it is a head-on attack on the twin beliefs that football is a man's game, and that no woman can possibly understand it. Or enjoy it.

Bah, humbug.

Right now, you may think that the "free safety" is on parole, and that Meg is a member of a royal family. At the end of this book, you will know otherwise.

But most important, I hope you will be able to watch pro football—whether in the stadium or on the tube—without being overwhelmed, and totally free from the illogical feeling that it is exclusively *his* game.

It's a game that both of you can enjoy, together.

And wouldn't it be nice (just once, of course) to tell him something about a play that he overlooked?

Also, since no wife is entirely free from the pro-football expertise of her husband, *my* husband has offered occasional comments and observations which appear as footnotes at the bottom of a page, or at the end of a chapter. And since he *is* a pro-football quarterback, you can use his comments to reinforce your position during the inevitable (friendly) arguments that you'll have with *your* husband.

ACKNOWLEDGMENTS

The authors wish to express their thanks to all those who contributed their advice and encouragement, and especially to James Kensil, Executive Director, Office of Professional Football; Art McNally, Supervisor NFL Officials; and Elinor Upton, who translated ideas into manuscript.

A Wife's Guide to Pro Football

The Game

Offering a definition of a pro-football game is a little like asking someone for a favorite recipe. The one you get from a short-order cook will be brief and simple; the one you get from a master chef will be elaborate. A football fan may see his (or her) favorite game as two groups of eleven men each running around the field. Or the game can be compared to some great battle—a martial chess match replete with grand strategy and subtle tactics.

The Field

No matter how it is defined, or by whom, football is played on a rectangular field 100 yards long, 53.3 yards wide. The long sides of the rectangle are sidelines. At each of the narrow ends of the field are goal posts, which look rather like the letter Y flattened out. (If you went to a college football game, you may recall that the goal posts looked like the letter H. Also, in pro football the goal posts are nudging the goal line; in college, they're on the end line, 10 yards behind the goal line. These are just two of the differences between college and pro football, some of which are significant, others not terribly important.)

Behind each goal post, at either end of the playing field, is the end zone. Broadly and briefly speaking, the object of a football game is to run or pass the football into the end zone of your opponents, while denying them entry to your end zone. The end zone is 10 yards long and, of course, the same width as the rest of the field. Two other bits of nomenclature: The point at which the end zone meets the playing field is the goal line, the crossing of which by the team you root for is devoutly to be wished. Parallel and opposite the goal line on the other side of the goal post—the flattened Y, remember?—is the end line, which marks the limit of the end zone. Everything else is out of bounds; i.e., not part of the playing field or end zone.

Before the teams begin playing, a football field should be a pretty sward of green grass and white stripes. The sidelines, goal lines, end zones, and end lines are marked in white. Within the playing-field area, a white (yard) line runs from sideline to sideline every 5 yards. In between are two sets of four short white lines, called hash marks, which measure distance yard by yard between the full-length stripes. The hash marks are 20 yards in from the sidelines.

Every 10 yards, a little sign in the out-of-bounds area announces the yard line. Beginning at either end of the field, the signs read: 10; 20; 30; 40;

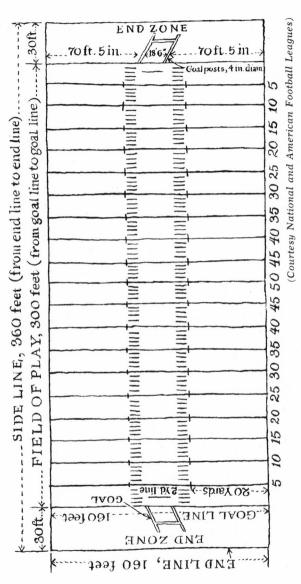

END ZONE

SIDE LINE, 360 feet (from end line to end line)

FIELD OF PLAY, 300 feet (from goal line to goal line)

30 ft.

70 ft. 5 in. — 18'6" — 70 ft. 5 in.

Goal posts, 4 in. diam.

5 10 15 20 25 30 35 40 45 50 45 40 35 30 25 20 15 10 5

20 yards — 2 yd. line

160 feet

GOAL LINE

GOAL

END ZONE

END LINE, 160 feet

30 ft.

(Courtesy National and American Football Leagues)

Fig. 1. Diagram of the Field

50; 40 (Notice this?); 30; 20; 10. Small flags mark the goal lines at both ends of the field.

Even though the entire football field is 100 yards long, it is sometimes measured and often referred to in terms of two 50-yard halves. One 50-yard half is the "property" of one team, the other half belongs to their opponents. Your team's half of the field is the one opposite to the direction in which your team is moving.

We now come to one of the most hallowed phrases in all of footballdom: the line of scrimmage. You probably think of a line as something you can see, something permanent. This one isn't. But it is central to the game of football. So, let us huddle together and backtrack just a bit.

The Four Downs and the Line of Scrimmage

When a team has the ball (has possession) it MUST advance the ball at least 10 yards to maintain possession.

The team with the ball has four chances—called downs—to move at least 10 yards. If the team does *not* advance the ball 10 yards in four downs, the ball "goes over" to its opponents—who then have four downs to move 10 yards.

The point on the field where the ball is first put down to begin the attempt to move it the required 10 yards—no matter where on the field that point is—is the line of scrimmage. And that imaginary line moves forward (and sometimes backward) with the ball.

One of the things that makes football seem confusing is the shorthand which is commonly used to describe any and all parts of the game. For example, the Blue team is playing the Red team. If the Blue team has gotten possession of the ball on its 20-yard line (that is, 80 yards away from a touchdown: 30 yards of Blue territory and all 50 yards of their opponents'), the situation could be described as, "First down and 10 yards to go from the Blue 20." However, you will be more likely to hear it as, "Blue's ball, first and 10 from their 20."

Now let us suppose that the Blue team has a first and 10 from their 35—that is, by way of review, first down and 10 yards to go from the Blue 35-yard line. The Blue team tries a running play, but its opponents hold it to *no gain*—literally, the Blues have not gained in their attempt to advance the ball 10 yards. The Blues now have their second chance to do that—their *second down*.

This time, the Blue team moves (advances) the ball 2 yards, to the Blue 37-yard line.

How would you sum up the situation?

If you answered, "Blue ball on their own 37, third down and 8 yards to go," or, "Blue ball on their 37, third and 8" you are no longer a rookie fan.

New math or not, the Blues had to make 10 yards. On first down, they were held to no gain. On second down, they gained 2 yards (of the needed 10 yards). Thus, two downs have been used up, and 10 minus 2 = 8 yards still to be gained.

The important things to remember are:

1. A team has four chances (downs) to make 10 yards or more.
2. If a team does this, it is said to have

achieved a (new) first down, and the cycle of downs required to make a first down begins all over again.

3. The line of scrimmage is where the ball is when it is put in play.

Suppose the Blue team is in a first and 10 situation on its own 35. The Blues, heroes all, move the ball 15 yards on their first try. The Blue team is now first and 10 from the 50-yard line.* The line of scrimmage—where the ball is—is the 50. The Blue team again has a "first and 10 situation," and the combative cycle begins once again.

Watching the Game

The best way to learn about pro football is to watch the game. At this point in your evolution as a fan, the chances of your husband giving you one of his hard-to-get tickets are pretty slim. Even if he did, he might grow increasingly grumpy if you asked questions that distracted him from the action on the field.

So begin by watching pro football on TV, preferably on a color set. Not only will the camera bring you close to the action, but TV's instant replay—via video tape—gives you an opportunity to rewatch important plays, or to follow the performance of an individual player who has done something splendid—or unsplendid.

When a pro-football team is playing at home, the game will be blacked out on local television. But listening to the game on radio can pay

*Regardless of what my favorite fan says, don't refer to this as the 50-yard line. It is "the 50"—sometimes referred to by broadcasters as "the mid-field stripe."

dividends, too. A radio announcer, unlike a TV sportscaster, must describe the football game without benefit of an accompanying picture. Naturally, the radio description of the game will be more complete verbally, and in the process, many of the questions posed by a beginning fan will be answered.

Pre-Game Activity

Let's suppose you are in the stadium. If you arrive an hour or so before game time, you'll see both teams warming up—performing group calisthenics, the quarterbacks limbering up their passing arms, the punter and field-goal kickers (about whom more later) practicing their specialties. After a while, both teams leave the field.

By now the stadium is almost full. As the big clock on the scoreboard moves toward game time, a mixture of tension and exhilaration—the uncertain expectancy of sweet victory or bitter defeat—ripples across the stands.

The Officials

Shortly before the game is to begin, a group of white-capped officials wanders onto the field. (They always enter together, perhaps from a sense of self-protection.)*

*Occasionally, almost every player feels that the good guys don't always wear white hats.

Pro football is played under the supervision of five officials: a referee, an umpire, a linesman, a field judge, and a back judge. The referee has general responsibility for controlling the game. His normal posi-

The Teams

The public-address system squawks to life, and the starting players of the visitors—the out-of-town team—are announced individually. One by one they appear from beneath the grandstand, sprint underneath the goal posts, and line up on the field. At this point there is much knowing conversation in the stands, because the decision as to which team will kick off and which team will receive will then be evident—the choice, arrived

---

tion is behind the team on offense. He has the final authority over the ball's position and progress. One of his duties is to explain to the team captains any option or alternatives to which their teams may be entitled.

The umpire has jurisdiction over the equipment and conduct of the players. He usually stands behind the team on defense. He is particularly responsible for noting any illegal play.

The linesman is primarily concerned with jurisdiction over the neutral zone (between the lines of the offensive and defensive teams) and infraction of the scrimmage formation. He marks the progress of the ball and directs assistants who handle the yardage chain on the sideline. His normal position is at one side of the field on a line with the neutral zone—the narrow area as wide as the football itself between the opposing offensive and defensive lines.

The field judge is responsible for timing the game. He starts and stops the game clock. He and the back judge, who works with him, are alert to rule on downfield play, sounding the whistle when the ball becomes dead. The normal position of the field judge is on the side of the field opposite the linesman. The position of the back judge is beyond the neutral zone, downfield.

at by a toss of a coin, having been determined some minutes previously, out of sight of the fans. If the visiting team's defensive players appear for the initial introduction the home team will have won the toss—it is generally considered good to begin by receiving the kickoff, and thereby have a chance to score first.

Regardless of whether the visiting team's offensive or defensive players are announced first, as soon as the starting eleven players are gathered together on the field they will break to their team's bench—literally, a long wooden bench, often sunk in a slight hollow to keep the players from blocking the view of the fans in ground-level seats. The rest of the team then jogs onto the field and is reunited with the starting eleven.

Now the home team's starting players, whether offensive or defensive, are introduced. Although the visiting players are sometimes greeted with cheers or boos, they are largely ignored—with the exception of a particularly detested opponent, or an outstanding one. The introduction of the home team's players is usually the signal for a chorus of applause and cheering—though if the fans feel that a player has done badly they won't hesitate to boo him, despite the fact that he is "theirs."

The Fans

I remember that a couple of years ago Jane Morrall, the wife of Earl Morrall, then a quarterback with the Giants, was sitting in Yankee Stadium. Jane and her son, Matt, endured a long and agonizing first half. The Giants were not playing well, and a highly vocal minority of the

60,000 who packed the stadium put the blame on Morrall. One particularly leather-lunged man was sitting right behind Jane and Matt. He welcomed Morrall by calling him a bum, and thereafter catalogued what he considered to be the quarterback's professional inadequacy in ever harsher terms. On the last play of the half, Morrall threw a long pass to a Giant player. It should have gone for a touchdown but, as sometimes happens, the intended receiver dropped the ball. The disenchanted fan ignored the receiver's error and directed another torrent of abuse at the downcast Morrall, who was slowly walking off the field.

Jane Morrall, who had been biting her lip as she listened to the man's tirade, could stand it no longer. She turned, and putting her arm around Matt's shoulders, quietly said, "You're talking about his father."

At Yankee Stadium, the silence that followed the noise rang like a bell. You have to give that fan some credit. He didn't show up for the second half of the game.

Football fans have a quixotic love/hate relationship with their team. Or maybe they simply feel that the price of the ticket entitles them to abuse a player or coach whenever they want. It seems strange to me that a fan who acts as did the one described above still considers himself a loyal supporter of the team he has been excoriating. I don't pretend to understand all the interplay between a fan and his team. And I freely admit to viewing this with a less than unprejudiced eye—after all, my husband is on the field. But it does seem to me that fans should encourage rather than discourage their team. Though most players will deny it, I am sure that fan support does have an effect on how the players perform.*

Anyway, back to the game. With both teams assembled at their benches, one of the officials meets with the captains of both teams, and they re-enact the toss of the coin. Each team huddles around its coach for a brief meeting—for last-minute words of warning or encouragement. Then the eleven defensive players and eleven offensive players take their positions on the field.

The Kickoff

The team which will kick off—essentially a defensive team—lines up along its 40-yard line. The football is mounted on a little plastic support —the kicking tee. An official blows on a whistle, makes a sweeping gesture with his arm; and the kicker, who has been lurking 5 yards or so back of his ten teammates, moves toward the ball in

*It does indeed. Pro football requires that a player perform to the absolute maximum of his potential on every play. As the game wears on, as muscles ache and reflexes slow, the support of the fans can supply badly needed adrenaline. Sometimes the booing and catcalls of dissatisfied fans can enrage a team—make it so angry that it rises to the challenge of the game in a spirit of "we'll show those so and so's in the stands." It is true, at least in something more than principle, that the fierce pride of the players—in themselves and their team—is central to their performance on the field. But support, or the lack of it, from fans certainly has an effect on a team, and on the quality of football it plays.

short stiff strides and boots it. As soon as the ball is touched by a member of the receiving team, it is "in play."

Meanwhile, the team which will receive has arranged itself. In general, five men will be on their 40-yard line, four more on the 20*, and two men—the deep receivers, one of whom will usually catch the kickoff—will be standing on their goal line.

The ball goes sailing through the air while beneath its calm flight the battle rages. The defensive team's objective is to contain the receiving team—to keep it far back in its own territory —and thereby avoid a long runback. The best way to achieve this is to kick the ball deep—if possible, into the end zone or beyond. If this happens, the receiving team puts the ball into play on its 20-yard line. This is called a touchback. If the kickoff receiver catches the ball in the end zone and feels that he can't run the ball successfully he will drop to one knee, thereby agreeing to a touchback. But if he thinks he can return the ball beyond his 20, he will try to run the ball. His teammates will attempt to set up a wall of blockers; that is, they will try to seal off the runner from the advancing kickoff team.

The kickoff is a moment of high excitement for the fans, and of special importance for the teams. It is a time of opportunity for the runner who receives the kick, and of danger for the team which kicks off. What happens on the kickoff can

---

*These four men form the *blocking wedge*. Their function is to wedge open a crevice between the oncoming defenders through which the kickoff receiver can escape.

have tremendous psychological impact on both teams. A good runback will make scoring a touchdown more likely, of course, but it also provides an enormous emotional lift, an added injection of confidence. Even to the apprentice eye, there is something beautiful in the kickoff return; the receiver catches the ball and, as though propelled by the release of taut springs, rockets forward. He feints left and right, searching for an opening—a hole—amid the bright-colored jerseys of the defenders. If he sees a hole, he will accelerate with unbelievable speed. In a flash he's through— hurtling toward the opposing goal line as his pursuers fling themselves in the air in desperate attempts to knock him off his feet.

More likely though, for all his hip-twisting evasion, for all his frightened-deer speed, someone will reach out and knock him down. When that happens, the referee signals the end of the play on his whistle and carefully positions the ball at the point at which the receiver was tackled. Most of the personnel who participated on both kicking and receiving teams stream off the field.

The team that kicked off sends in its defensive unit. The team with the ball sends in its offensive unit. The latter form a huddle, a rough circle of helmeted warriors. A play is called by the quarterback, and with a simultaneous clap of hands—an aural ritual of confidence in themselves and the oneness of their team—the players break the huddle and go to the line.

It is time for the call of the quarterback.

The Offense

There are few sports in which team play is as important as it is in football. Eleven men must react as one, each making an individual contribution to the success of all. But there is one player from whom more is demanded than the others: the quarterback. Before the wives of other players race to their typewriters to dash off a stinging rebuttal, I again want to emphasize that no quarterback can succeed without the total support of his teammates. Thus having mollified the loyal opposition, let's see how and why the role of the quarterback is so important.

On a table near the living-room window of our house lies a black loose-leaf notebook. The penalty for losing this innocuous-looking volume is $500. It is the New York Giants play book—a collection of the forty ways in which the Giants have practiced moving the ball. Each play is diagramed to show the individual assignment of every player;

whom he must block, where he must run. One thing all these plays have in common: they begin with the ball being snapped to the quarterback.

The Interior Linemen

One of the rules of football is that the offensive team must have seven men (only) on the line of scrimmage. The man in the very center of the line is called, appropriately enough, the center. It is he, crouched over the ball, who levers it swiftly back through his legs to the quarterback—a movement accomplished with swift, sharp movements of the wrists, the *snap* of the ball.

On either side of the center are the guards— right guard and left guard. Next to each guard is a tackle, also specified by right and left—that is, to the right or left of the center, a matter of geographical position having nothing to do with politics.

These five offensive players—two tackles, two guards, the center—are the *interior linemen*. They block for runners and provide pass blocking against onrushing defensive players when the quarterback wants to throw.*

*Blocking means just what it sounds like: preventing the opposition from reaching the ball carrier or quarterback. While blocking, the offensive linemen are not allowed to use their hands, only their forearms, head, shoulders, and upper torso. Blocking on the line for a running play means moving somebody out of the way.

Pass blocking means preventing the defenders from reaching the QB—usually by forming a protective

The interior linemen are a quarterback's best friends. They provide the precious seconds of respite from the thundering herd of the defensive linemen whose joyful purpose is to dismember the QB or, chortling gleefully, throw themselves on him in an unrelenting effort to pound him into the ground. The "average" defensive lineman in pro football must break the scale at around 260 pounds, and some weigh 300 or more. My husband burdens the scale hardly at all: 190 pounds.

The Ends

The last man on the right side of the offensive line is the tight end. He has a dual assignment: to block on running plays, and to catch passes. He is called "tight" not because he has a drinking problem, but because he usually lines up shoulder to shoulder with the right tackle, tight against the right tackle, as it were. In some formations the tight end will line up left, in which case he is shoulder to shoulder with the left tackle.

On the other (left) end of the line is the split end (SE). But instead of rubbing shoulders with the left tackle, he is separated from him by a gap of several yards. He is, in effect, "split" from the rest of the line. The split end can block, but his prime mission is to catch passes.

---

circle, or cup, around him. If you watch the feet of the offensive-pass blockers, you will often notice them executing what appears to be a series of dance steps. This helps keep the incoming (defensive) rush off stride, which means more time for the QB.

I love my interior line.

The Backs

There are now seven offensive players accounted for, which means you must learn the positions of only four more. One of these is the quarterback. He stands immediately behind the center. A yard or so behind the quarterback (QB) are the halfback (HB) and the fullback (FB). Both these players can carry the ball on running plays, block for each other or the quarterback, or be sent downfield as receivers on pass plays.

The eleventh offensive player is the flanker back (FL). He is a pass receiver who can be positioned to the right of the tight end, separated by a few yards, or in the gap between the split end and the left tackle.*

The arrangement of the players described above, and diagramed in Figure 2, is a very simple, very basic pro-football formation. (For variations of the basic offensive formation see Appendix.) Football teams are constantly experi-

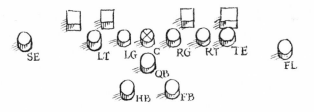

Fig. 2. The Basic Offensive Formation

*Remember that only seven offensive players can be at the line of scrimmage, so the flanker must be one yard behind; i.e., inside, the line of scrimmage.

menting with variations in formation. On different downs a team may use different formations because one formation may be easier to run from, another easier to pass from. And field position—how near or far the team is from their own and their opponent's goal line—can influence the choice of formation.

The Call of the Play

Now let's return to the quarterback. The team breaks the huddle and moves to the line of scrimmage. The quarterback, standing behind and leaning forward over the center's back, begins his call, a code of numbers and/or colors and other word symbols which tells the offense when to execute the agreed-upon play. Here is a sample QB call:

"Set."

At this word all the offensive players hunker down with their hands on their knees.

"Two."

Every member of the team except the quarterback freezes in a three-point stance—the ritual football crouch, the weight of the body comfortably supported on the haunches, feet planted firmly in the turf, one arm vertical to the field and just touching the ground.

One second has now passed, and the man in motion—if there is one—is now permitted to move.*

*The rules allow one backfield player to be in *motion*. That player—a halfback, fullback, or flanker back—can move parallel to the line of scrimmage behind his own line. He cannot cross the line, of course, until the ball is snapped. When a sportscaster

"Forty."

Nothing happens.

"Ready."

Nothing happens.

"Hut. Hut."

Action. You can hear the deep grunting as the offensive line moves off the ball, exploding into the defenders and driving them backward and away from the play. Simultaneously, the quarterback pivots around and shovels the ball to the fullback, who is charging by. Legs pumping, the fullback bulldozes through a hole in the defense that has briefly appeared between the offensive team's left tackle and left guard.

To understand what the QB said, pretend that we eavesdropped on the huddle and heard the QB call, "Slant 34 on two."

Each back has a code number. For example, 2 for the halfback and 3 for the fullback. The holes —the openings to be made between each of the linemen as they block, forcing specified defenders away from the ball carrier—are also numbered. The hole numbers start at center, zero, with even numbers to the left (the shorter or weak) side and odd numbers to the right (the longer or strong) side of the line.

In this call, the QB uses a single-digit number followed by a two-digit number. The one-digit number, "Two," indicates that the play agreed upon in

---

says "So-and-so is in motion to the right," or simply "Man in motion to the right," it means that one of the backs is moving—at a trot—behind the line of scrimmage toward the right sideline. The same reference to motion to the left means a similar action toward the left sideline.

the huddle still stands. The two-digit number, "Forty," is camouflage. "Ready" alerts the team to the upcoming snap. If the QB had specified only one hut—"Slant 34 on one"—the center would have snapped the ball on the first hut.

What is Slant 34? It is a running play in which the number 3 back, the FB, will carry the ball through the number 4 hole, the one between the weak (left)-side guard and tackle.

Conversely, Slant 23 would mean the number 2 back, the HB, carries the ball through the number 3 hole—between the strong (right)-side guard and tackle.

The Audible

A team has only thirty seconds from the sound of the referee's whistle to huddle, go to the line of scrimmage, and get the play off. Now suppose that while the QB is calling signals he notices that the defense has shifted in such a way as to make it unwise to call the play he originally intended. He then *audibles**—that is, through coded signals he

*An audible—changing the call at the line of scrimmage—is sometimes referred to as an *automatic*. Here is an example: "Set. One. Forty. Ready. Hut. Hut." The original call was for slant 34 on two. But by calling "One" the QB signals that the next number— coded to stand for a passing play, for example—will replace whatever play he called in the huddle. "Forty" is that new play. Note that the snap count—whether on one, two, or three "huts"—remains the same as the snap count for the original play agreed upon in the huddle.

To keep the defense guessing, the automatic num-

tells his teammates that he is canceling the play called in the huddle and is substituting another.

You don't have to understand the QB's system of coded signals. An awful lot of male fans don't. But it is engrossing evidence of the complicated, chess-game quality of pro football. (It also might be fun to see if your husband knows what the signals mean.)

The Quarterback in Action

When the ball is snapped, the QB will do one of three things: hand off to the HB or FB; pass to one of the ends or a back; run with the ball himself.

On a running play the QB will either hand off or pitch out. The former means he literally pushes the football into the tummy of a HB or FB rushing by; the latter is an underhanded toss of the ball to a running back farther away.

Since the coded plays for pro football are top secret, there's not much point in trying to learn the distinction between Slant 34 and Counter 20. But you will hear running plays described in a more general football argot. A *sweep*, or *power sweep*, means a running play that goes wide; that is, around the end and close to the sideline. Almost inevitably; this play requires the guards to *pull*.

---

ber is changed from game to game, and sometimes a completely different range of numbers—10 to 20— or colors—red, blue—are used to conceal from the defense and reveal to the offense that the QB has audibled or automaticked.

The Pulling Guards

The guards, though big men by almost every standard, are not the biggest linemen in football. Although they may weigh 240 to 260 pounds, they must be quick, mobile. On a play such as a sweep, at the snap the guards move laterally behind the line of scrimmage and provide blocking in advance of the runner who is attempting to circle the end. That movement out of the line is what is meant by pulling.

The Power Play

A straight ahead, or power play, is exactly what the words suggest: the ball carrier moves straight ahead and depends on the brute force of the linemen to shoulder defenders out of the way.*

Trap Blocking

Trap blocking mixes deceit with power. Instead of blocking the defender directly ahead of him, a right tackle or guard will block the defender usually handled by the left tackle or guard. Meanwhile, the left tackle or guard is blocking farther downfield. As a result, the incoming (defending) lineman is blocked from an unexpected direction, which can create a massive hole. This maneuver

*As a verb, shoulder is pretty colorful. But pro-football linemen are taught to use their heads, literally. The lineman tries to drive his helmet into a defender's chest. Then, if the defender begins to slide off the block, the lineman still has a chance to hold up the defender with a shoulder.

requires practice and the kind of instinctive timing that offensive linemen acquire by playing together as a unit. *Trap plays* are simply running plays through the interior line—from left tackle to right tackle—which depend on trap blocking.

The Reverse

A reverse is a guileful play in which one player who is apparently going to run with the ball hands off to another player who then moves in the opposite direction. For example, the QB hands off to the halfback. The HB begins running to his left. Suddenly the split end turns around and begins running toward the HB, who hands off to the SE. The SE then keeps running in an attempt to circle around the opposite side of the line—past the tight end—and scampers down the sideline. Any time a ball carrier goes round the end, someone is sure to say "he turned the corner."

The Draw Play

A draw play is equally deceitful, but in another way. After the snap, the QB gives every appearance that he is going to pass. After this bit of theatricalism, he hands off to the HB or FB, who has been standing by looking unconcerned. The back then scoots ahead through holes the defenders have left in their frantic attempts to reach the QB.

A pro-football team usually has the ball for about sixty plays during a game. Of these perhaps thirty-five will be running plays, and twenty-five will be passing plays.

The Pass

A quarterback is described as either a roll-out or pocket passer. In the roll-out, the QB will move laterally behind the line of scrimmage. He can pass on the run, or suddenly stop and throw. A pocket passer won't fit in your purse. The appellation comes from the kind of protection he gets, the "pocket" of blocking which his linemen form around him. A QB who stays more or less in the same general area behind the line is a pocket passer. After the snap, the QB will usually retreat 7 or so yards, running backward, then stop. This is called *dropping back*, or fading back.

Almost all passes are forward. That is, the ball is thrown to a receiver who is in front of the quarterback and usually, although not always, across the line of scrimmage.*

Once again, rather than deal in all the subtleties of passing, try to recognize the terms and

*The one kind of pass which isn't forward is a *lateral*. A lateral is a pass thrown to a receiver *behind* the passer. Most (but not all) laterals occur on the other side of the line of scrimmage—in the territory of the defense—when a player about to be tackled laterals to a teammate. A lateral can also occur behind the line of scrimmage. In our 1968 game against the New Orleans Saints I was about to be thrown for a loss and I lateraled to Willie Young, our 270-pound offensive-left tackle. The "Sugar Bear," as we call him, ran for a short gain and afterward innocently inquired whether there were any openings in our backfield.

The danger of the lateral is that although when a forward pass falls incomplete only the down is lost, an uncaught lateral is a free ball—meaning that if the defense recovers it the other team gets possession.

plays that you will most often see or hear described.

Pass Patterns

The first thing to remember is that just as the offensive linemen (including the ends) have very specific blocking assignments for running plays, the pass receivers have routes on the field that they follow during passing plays. These routes are called *patterns*. Most passing plays are known by the pattern that a receiver ran on the field.

A *square-out* means the receiver went a predetermined number of yards toward the enemy goal line and made a 90-degree turn towards the right or left sideline.

On a *down-and-in* pattern the receiver goes downfield 5 to 10 yards and cuts at a 45-degree angle inside—toward the middle of the field.

A *post* pattern is a deep down-and-in. The receiver moves far downfield and cuts diagonally in toward the goal post.

A *sideline* pattern is usually run by the SE or other wide receiver and is designed to pick up first-down yardage. The receiver goes downfield 5 to 20 yards, hesitates, fakes coming back toward the line of scrimmage, and scampers to either sideline.

A pass *over the middle* is precisely that; a receiver is more or less in the middle of the field and, by inference, in the middle of the original formation that the defenders had.

A *fly* pattern is a touch of hysterical beauty. It means a receiver—almost always one of great speed—runs as far and as fast as he can. The quarterback throws the ball as far as he can, and the receiver runs under the ball. This has also become known as *throwing the bomb*.

A *flare* pass is one thrown to a receiver behind the line of scrimmage close to the sidelines. Sometimes this is called a *safety-valve pass*—referring to the fact that the QB wanted to pass to someone else, but the defenders made it impossible to do so.

In the *screen pass* the entire offensive team turns actor. The QB drops back his normal 7 yards—and then retreats another 4 or 5. Meanwhile, the offensive line, which has been holding its blocks for 2 or 3 counts—mentally ticking off "one thousand and one; one thousand and two"— then allows the defenders to filter through it toward the QB. The QB then flips the ball to a HB or FB who is on the other—downfield—side of the screen of onrushing defenders. When the HB or FB catches the pass he yells "Go" and moves ahead, preceded by the offensive linemen who have moved over to provide blocking. Unless the defensive players are fooled into believing that they are really penetrating the offensive line—and not just being allowed in—the screen pass won't work. One sign of its failure appears when a defender yells "Screen, screen" as a warning to his less perceptive teammates.

You will sometimes hear of the QB that "he circled a back." This refers to sending the HB or FB as a pass receiver in a wide arc around either end and into the middle—really in a half circle. And you will certainly hear receivers described as having "good hands" and/or "good moves." The former means that the receiver has an uncanny ability to catch any pass thrown near him, the latter refers to the ability of the receiver to fool the defender by faking—either by a movement of head, shoulders, feet, or even eyes—that he is going to move in one direction, while in actuality he immediately veers off in another. One result of having "good moves" is that a receiver is "open"—uncovered by his defender and in an optimum position to receive the QB's pass. A completed pass is called a *reception*, as in "Smith makes the reception on the 40-yard line."

Although a QB does 99 per cent of a team's passing, one of the backs occasionally throws the ball. This is the *halfback option* or *fullback option* —meaning that the back has the choice of running with the ball if he has a clear field ahead, or of throwing to a receiver.

Finally, it is now increasingly common to hear of the *play-action pass*, or of *play-fake passing*. They mean the same thing, namely that the QB sends a back into the line on what appears to be a running play, while another back or receiver is weaving his way into position to catch a pass—which is what the QB had in mind all the time.*

The Quarterback Run

As previously mentioned, there are times when the QB himself runs with the ball. Most commonly, these occur when the needed yardage is a matter of inches, or when it is unwise to attempt a hand-off. In such situations the QB usually moves

*Passing off of a faked running play tends to "freeze" the defense, slowing down their response and enabling a receiver to get clear who might otherwise have been covered by a defender.

straight ahead, trying to insinuate himself between the defenders. This is called a *quarterback sneak*, and is by no means a characterization of the player himself.

Another occasion for the quarterback carrying the ball has an equally misleading name: *bootleg*. In such instances, the offensive unit is close to its opponent's goal line. The defense, as the sportscasters are wont to say, "is packed in solidly"— meaning that with so little ground behind them, the defenders can concentrate on putting up a solid wall of beef and muscle. In such circumstances, it is often extremely difficult for a normal running play to work, and the receivers too have only limited room in which to run their patterns. This is the moment for the bootleg: the quarterback fakes a hand-off to the HB or FB and, hoping that the defenders won't spy the ball he is hiding on his hip, sets off on a sweeping run around end. There is, of course, a bootleg left or right—but no wrong.

Some quarterbacks run with greater frequency (and success) than others. My husband has earned the soubriquet "Scrambler" from his artful dodging hither and yon. In his case, the nickname refers not only to his willingness to run with the ball as an offensive tactic but also to his frequent twisting-and-turning sideline-to-sideline evasion of defensive linemen. Because he is smaller and faster than his pursuers he can usually elude them, but every so often he gets dumped by a behemoth. At such times I utter a prayer for his health and give thanks for Blue Cross.

In theory, every play that a QB calls should result in a touchdown.* But this assumes a level of precision beyond mortals—even jumbo-sized ones like football players. There are times, as I have occasionally observed while watching the Giants, when the offense does not move the ball. A first-down run gains no yardage. A second-down sweep is held to no gain. A third-down pass falls incomplete. It is then fourth down and time to *punt*.

The Punt

At such times, a kicking specialist is called upon to boot the ball to the defenders who will, upon receiving the punt, then switch to the offense. Although punting means, by definition, giving up possession and therefore an opportunity to score, there are many times when it is safer to punt— and give the ball to the opposition far away from your own goal—than to try a fourth-down play. For if the fourth down is unsuccessful, the opposition will then have possession wherever that fourth-down play was stopped. Of course, if the fourth down *is* successful, your team then has a first down, but the risk far outweighs the possible gain.

The Field Goal

On other occasions, the offense may drive to within field-goal range of their opponent's goal. The field-goal kicker (who may or may not be the team's punter as well) is a specialist who can boot

*And so they do—that is, during the team's practice.

the football over the crossbar and between the up-rights of the goal post. It is not uncommon for to-day's expert toes to kick field goals of 40 or more yards. The field goal is worth three points.

The Extra Point

In addition to the touchdown (six points) and the field goal, a team can score by a *conversion*. After a touchdown, the scoring team has an opportunity to kick the ball through the uprights from its opponent's 2. Thus, a conversion is just like a field goal, except that it occurs only after a touchdown and counts for one point.*

Defensive Scoring

Although the offense does most of a team's scoring, the defense can score, too, in three ways. We'll examine two of those ways now, because they are the results of "errors" by the offense.

The Interception

Sometimes a QB's throw is inaccurate, or perhaps his intended receiver has slipped on wet ground. Regardless of the reason, there are occasions when the defense manages an *interception* —a catch in the air of a pass thrown by the offense. Not infrequently, the defender who makes the interception weaves his way across the goal line. This is a moment of special satisfaction for

*In the American Football League a team may also attempt a two-point conversion by running or passing across the goal line from the 2-yard line.

the defender, and of chagrin and embarrassment for the offending quarterback.

The Fumble

In other situations, the offensive team may *fumble*. This means that the football, which has been handled with easy familiarity, suddenly develops the properties of a red-hot hand grenade coated with grease and covered with needles. In short, someone drops the ball. And if a defender recovers the fumble he can run for a touchdown.

The Clock

A football game is divided into four fifteen-minute quarters—sometimes called periods—which are themselves coupled to form two halves.

At the end of each quarter the teams change goals. Suppose your team is moving east to west and has the ball on its own 35, and the first quarter ends. The two teams then swap goals. Your team is now moving west to east and has retained possession on its own 35—the 35 that was, during the first quarter, the enemy's.

When the first half ends, both teams go to their respective locker rooms for a twenty-minute respite. At the beginning of the second half, the team that received the kick when the game began now kicks off.

Besides struggling with the defenders, the offensive team sometimes fights against the tyranny of the clock—for example, when they are losing.

Although a game consumes sixty minutes of actual playing time, you are undoubtedly (and perhaps painfully) aware that one game can occupy your husband's attention for most of an afternoon. This is because the actual playing time —the time during which game action takes place —starts and stops according to the flow of action on the field. For example, an incomplete pass, or a completed pass to a receiver who goes out of bounds (across the sidelines), stops the official clock. But a completed pass to a receiver who is tackled on the playing field allows the clock to keep running. Obviously, a team which is inches away from a touchdown when the first half ends gets no advantage from being so close (and yet so far) from a score.

Time is such an important element in football that every professional team practices a two-minute drill. This special exercise is cued by the warning which the officials give both teams when two minutes remain in the half. The two-minute drill is designed to give practice in conserving the official time clock. The usual device is to throw a sideline pass that enables the receiver to escape across the sideline, thus stopping the clock. In addition, a team is allowed three time-outs per half, which are often saved for the last two minutes since, of course, they also stop the clock.

From the opening kickoff to the final gun, pro-football players are believers—in themselves. Indeed, they have to be. As has often been said, one pro-football team can beat any other on any given Sunday. Of course some teams are better than others, but mental attitude—the will to win—can compensate for a deficiency in personnel. If a team wants victory badly enough, and if they believe in themselves, they stand a good chance of achieving that victory.

Football players vary enormously in their post-game emotional reactions. It doesn't take much personal adjustment to live with victory. But a defeat can demoralize a team in strange and subtle ways. And no matter how hard a player tries to wipe out the memory of today's defeat and focus his attention on next week's game, there is a part of his mind that defies constructive mental discipline, that returns again and again to what might have been.

When the Giants are playing in New York I usually go to the game at Yankee Stadium. Afterwards, Fran and I often have dinner out. If the Giants lost, standing outside the locker room and chatting with the wives of other players is a prologue to tension. It is tension silently denied, but it is there.

Perhaps we'll have dinner with some of the other players and their wives, or alone. In either case, although football may be discussed, the recently concluded game will not. Even afterward, riding home in the car, the subject is studiously avoided.

When we get home, Fran may prowl nervously around the house. (One sign of this inner tension: He will open a soft drink, take a sip and put it down somewhere, open another bottle and leave that half finished, open still another—and so forth. The worse the defeat, the more intense this one-man relay race around the refrigerator becomes.)

When he finally comes to bed he'll lie there,

staring up at the ceiling, seeing against the plaster and white paint the images of what might have been, of third and inches and passes gone awry. Sometimes I try to break the mood, venturing a word of encouragement. More often than not he will seem to agree with me—adding that the loss is behind the team now, and that the important thing is next Sunday, the next game. But I know that he is still replaying the game, continuing to upbraid himself for plays gone wrong—the penance of a quarterback in defeat.

Because I am married to a quarterback I have a certain empathy with the offensive players on any team. For the same reason, I can't help regarding the players on the other side of the line of scrimmage as the villains of the piece. They are the cause of every quarterback's bad dreams.

Who they are and what they do is explored (without prejudice, I hope) in the next chapter.

The Defense

The defensive players in pro football think negatively. Theirs is an act of denial—to crush the quarterback before he passes, overwhelm a ball carrier before he gains yardage, punish a pass receiver with a vicious tackle that forces the ball from his grasp.

Just as the offensive team operates from a variety of formations—alignments of personnel—so does the defensive team. A basic defensive formation is shown in Figure 3.

The Front Four

Directly across the line of scrimmage from the offensive interior line are four defensive linemen, often called the *front four*. The two defensive players at either end of the line are (if you haven't already guessed) the right and left defensive ends (DE). The two linemen in the middle are the right and left defensive tackles (DT). Note that there

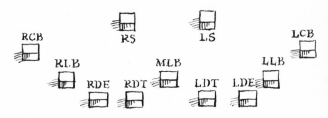

Fig. 3. The Basic Defensive Formation

is no such thing as a defensive center, nor are there defensive guards.

The Linebackers

Behind the four defensive linemen are three linebackers: the middle linebacker (MLB), the right linebacker (RLB), the left linebacker (LLB). The RLB and LLB overlap the defensive ends slightly, thus providing some defensive protection between the extremes of the offensive formation and the sidelines.

The Secondary

Behind the three linebackers are four more defensive players. They are generically referred to as defensive halfbacks, but each has a separate designation and specific duties. The two closest to the line of scrimmage, behind the right and left linebackers, are *cornerbacks*—identified as right (RCB) and left (LCB) cornerback. The last barriers between the team with the ball and a touchdown are the *safeties*. As with the cornerbacks, there is a right (RS) and a left (LS) safety. As a group, the four defensive backs are sometimes called the *secondary*—a reference, perhaps, to their representing the second (and last) line of defense.

Defensive Strategy

Just as the quarterback calls the signals for the offensive team, a defensive captain—almost always a player of many years of experience—calls signals for the defense. And just as the offensive team has a repertoire of plays, so the defensive team has an inventory of formations and options with which to frustrate the offense. We will examine some of these defensive techniques, but first let's look at the general responsibilities of the various elements of the defense.

The front four—the defensive ends and defensive tackles—have a dual mission: to demolish the quarterback if he tries to pass, and to squash running plays before they penetrate the line of scrimmage.

As was pointed out earlier, there are certain times in football when a pass is expected, as dictated by the down and by the yards which need to be gained in order to secure a first down. Third down is the classic passing down. This doesn't mean that a quarterback will *always* pass on third down, any more than that he *won't* pass on first or second down. But third down with anything more than 1 or 2 yards to go usually means a pass play.

The Job of the Front Four

Now if you and I know this, surely the defense does as well. So whenever the quarterback drops back to pass, or when it seems likely that he will pass, the defensive linemen execute their *pass rush*. The front four attempt to fight their way through the blocks of the offensive linemen and, in Chaucerian terms, smite the quarterback a mighty blow. The pass rush is also described as "pressuring the quarterback."

The front four must also guard against running plays. Again this means fighting off the blocks of the offensive linemen. Even if a defensive lineman is not being blocked, he still has a defensive responsibility that ends only when the referee's whistle signals that the play is over. For example, if the quarterback calls for an end run around the right side of his (offensive) line, the defensive right end—opposite the left offensive tackle—may be relatively unopposed. The blocking of the offensive line will be concentrated in the direction in which the ball carrier is moving; that is, around the right side of the offensive line.

If the defensive left end is keen and resourceful* he will, in the argot of the sportscasters, "trail the play," or show "great lateral movement,"

---

*As a quarterback, I have yet to encounter a defensive lineman who wasn't keen and resourceful. During the defensive-pass rush, you will probably notice that the onrushing linemen have their hands raised over their heads. Unfortunately, they aren't surrendering—just trying to block the quarterback's view of his receivers. And since the defensive linemen are often tall men—6 feet 5 inches or more—their upraised arms manage to block off a considerable portion of the horizon. In addition, some linemen yell as they struggle to reach the quarterback—a kind of growling "arrrgh" which may or may not be a vocal attempt to intimidate the quarterback.

or display good "pursuit." The first means that the left defensive end comes swiftly across the field behind the play and sneaks up on the ball carrier from his unprotected rear. "Great lateral movement" refers to the same player moving with equal swiftness across the field to get in front of the play. "Good pursuit" is really generalized praise of a lineman's mobility and aggressiveness.

You may occasionally hear that a lineman *submarined*. It doesn't mean the defensive player escaped beneath the turf, but that he torpedoed a running play by getting underneath an offensive block, thereby denying running room to the ball carrier. Proper (even if innocent) use of the word is well calculated to impress any male fan.

The Linebackers' Job

Backing up the front four are the linebackers. Should a ball carrier manage to penetrate the defensive line, the linebacker closest to the action must be prepared to come up to the play and stop the runner before he gains additional yardage. The linebackers must also be wary of pass receivers, particularly of a halfback or fullback coming out of the backfield. Often, one of the linebackers is *keyed* on a halfback or fullback; that is, wherever the designated HB or FB goes—right or left in the offensive formation—he is the responsibility of one particular linebacker.*

*Of course, if the QB knows which linebacker is keying on the HB or FB—something which becomes obvious during the game from the movement of the linebackers—he will use the keyed-upon player as a decoy. For example if the middle linebacker is keying

The Blitz

It is an often repeated maxim of football that the best pass defense is a good pass rush. So on likely passing situations—third down and long yardage, or any down on which penalties (about which more later) have aggravated the required yardage—the defense will maximize its pass rush. In addition to the rush of the front four, one or more of the linebackers—before the ball is snapped—will move up to the line of scrimmage in a position to join the pass rush. This is the *blitz*, or *red dog*, or just *dog*, as the players call it. It is another facet of the chess-game quality of football, the "what will you do if I do that, or if you think I'm going to do that" syndrome—a cycle of real and faked defensive shifts which is ended only by the snap of the ball. In order to confuse the QB, the linebackers may fake a blitz from one side and blitz from the other. Or the linebackers may fake a blitz and then retreat to their normal field position.*

---

on the fullback, perhaps the FB will be sent on a fake running play to the left side, while the real ball carrier, the HB, is sent up the middle—the area vacated by the MLB. By the time the middle linebacker realizes that he has been decoyed, the HB will have carried for a substantial gain.

*The offensive equivalent of the defense's changing its formation—by threatening a blitz, for example—is the quarterback's changing the play by calling an automatic at the line of scrimmage (see *The Offense*). The ability of the offense and defense to perceive each other's stratagems as reflected in their formations is sometimes called *reading*, as in, "The QB read the

The Secondary's Job

The cornerbacks and safeties are football's grey-hounds. To cover fleet-footed pass receivers, a defensive back needs phenomenal reflexes as well as great speed. One of the classic images of pro football is that of a pass receiver racing down the sideline with a defensive back matching him stride for stride. Overhead, the ball arcs downfield in a high spiral toward the sprinting pair. As one, they leap upward, arms straining for the ball. With a last desperate effort, the defender manages to tip the pigskin away and both men fall to the ground. As one gal said to me, "Football is an outdoor ballet." Well, at least some of the time.

Although I have specified the cornerbacks and safeties by right and left, they are often referred to as *strong* side and *weak* side. This isn't a matter of muscle. A defensive back is referred to as being "strong side" when he is playing on the side of the field where the offense has its strong side. (Remember? The offensive line has both a strong and weak side, the strong being the one terminating with the tight end.) And the flanker can be positioned on this side, too. If so, there is unequal offensive potential to this (strong) side and the defense, naturally, has to adjust. One way of compensating for the strong-side offensive formation is this: The strong side linebacker—in this case, the left linebacker—moves up to the line of scrimmage and becomes, in effect, a fifth defensive

---

defenses perfectly,"—and therefore called a play which capitalized on a change in the defensive formation.

lineman. Thus, the strong side linebacker is in a position to neutralize the tight end. This allows the strong-side cornerback (the left cornerback) to concentrate on the flanker, while the strong-side safety can watchfully await a back coming out of the backfield.*

Because an unbalanced line permits a diversity of plays, pro-football offensive lines inevitably have a strong and weak side.** Because of this, the defensive techniques developed to cope with unbalanced formations do not, as a rule, specify a

*I think you can see that the designations left linebacker, right linebacker, and middle linebacker are somewhat academic. What is important is whether the linebackers are playing the weak or strong side of the (offensive) line and, therefore, what each linebacker's defensive responsibilities are. To identify these, the defensive teams use a special code. On the Giants, for example, a trio of feminine names are used: Wanda (for the weak side linebacker); Meg (for the middle linebacker); Sarah (for the strong side linebacker). Thus the defensive players can quickly refer to the linebacker's position—eliminating the polysyllabic reference to middle linebacker, etc.

**Your husband will inform you that there are a couple of offensive formations which have a balanced line; that is, the split end moves in toward the left tackle and becomes a "tight end" (left). Such formations sacrifice passing flexibility for powerful blocking. They are rarely used in pro football except when the needed yardage is a matter of inches. Although the defense knows a running play is coming, the blocking advantages are such that the ball can often be advanced nonetheless. If you fail to recognize the formation, a sportscaster reminds you with this description: "Balanced line, tight T-formation." Sometimes this is abbreviated to "Tight-T."

right and left safety. They are now called *strong side* safety (SS) and free safety (FS). The cornerbacks, thank goodness, are still right and left.

Actually the nomenclature is—for once—quite explicit. Of the two men who are playing safety, one will always play as the strong-side safety. He will always be the last defender on the side of the field where the offense has its strong side. The strong-side safety is playing a man; his assignment may be the flanker, or a back coming out of the backfield who goes downfield beyond the territory of the cornerback. Depending on what offensive play has been called, his assignment will vary, but it will always entail coverage of someone.

Not so the free safety. The free safety plays the ball. If he sees a pass being thrown to a player going deep he will join the coverage of that player, or he may team with a linebacker on a pass over the middle, or come up to help stop a running play. The free safety roams the field, shadowing the ball.*

---

*One free safety who plays the ball with inspired freedom is Larry Wilson of the St. Louis Cardinals. Wilson is the innovator of the safety blitz, a tactic once the exclusive prerogative of linebackers. Because Wilson is fast, he can effectively threaten to blitz and still drop back to his normal position. And when he does blitz, the same speed often gets him through an offensive line unscathed—which is more than can be said for the unfortunate quarterback. However, remember that the added pass rush obtained by blitzing a linebacker or safety also means an equivalent reduction in defensive coverage. So if a quarterback suspects that a blitz is coming he will surely pass to a receiver whose pass pattern takes him into the territory deserted by the blitz. This is yet another quid pro quo in football's seesawing tactical struggle.

The Safety

Despite the fact that the defensive team's energies are concentrated on denying a score to the offense, the defenders can score points for their side in three ways. Two of these have been discussed earlier—the intercepted pass and the recovered fumble that are returned for touchdowns. The third way the defenders can get on the scoreboard is by a *safety*. A safety occurs when the defenders tackle an offensive player with the ball in the opposition's end zone.

The classic safety is achieved by tackling the punter (or QB) in his own end zone. Suppose The Enemy—we can always derive some satisfaction by inflicting adversity on *them*—has the ball; fourth down and 8 yards to go on their own 5-yard line. Clearly, they dare not try for a first down lest they fail and give possession to our stalwarts just 5 yards away from a touchdown. So the enemy has no alternative but to punt. The center snaps the ball to the punter, who is standing almost 10 yards deep in his end zone, hands outstretched before him. He receives the snap. The punter holds the ball in front of him, takes a stride forward, and is poised for the kick. But wait! One of our linemen has broken through and tackles the kicker in the end zone before he can get the kick away. We have scored a safety: two points for our side.*

*A safety is scored by tackling an offensive player who has *possession* of the football behind his own goal line. But if possession is surrendered, a touchdown is scored. For example, if the punter had actually kicked the ball, and it was blocked and the ball was recovered in the end zone by the defensive team, it would be a touchdown.

Not only have we scored, but our team will soon get possession of the ball. For the team which has given up the safety must free kick (punt) the ball to its opponent from its own 20.*

There'was a time when football fans concentrated their interest and enthusiasm on the offense. The appearance on the field of the defensive unit was a signal to seek out the nearest stadium vendor of hot dogs and soft drinks.

Today, although food and drink are as much a part of the stadium scene as ever, the defense has attained equal stature with the offense.** Outstanding defensive players share the charisma—and the glare of publicity—that was once the exclusive franchise of offensive players. One irrefutable evidence of this is the fine impartiality shown by youngsters seeking autographs. One such occasion stands out particularly.

I had taken my daughter, Angela, to watch the Giants practice at their training camp at Fairfield University in Connecticut. After the practice session was over, the players, limp with fatigue, began their charley-horsed walk back to the

*Remember that old saw about possession being nine-tenths of the law? In football, possession is 100 per cent. When a team has possession it not only has the opportunity to score points, but it is simultaneously denying that opportunity to its opponents. Thus, in a very real sense, the defensive team is an extension of the spirit of the offense. And even though an intercepted pass or recovered fumble may not result in a touchdown on that play, it does give the offense yet another chance to score.

**And rightly so. In fact, a great many pro-football coaches believe that the foundation of a strong football team is a solid defense.

gymnasium and the soothing comfort of hot show-
ers. Instantly, a horde of kids descended onto the
field, clustering around the players with hero
worship in their eyes and scraps of paper in their
hands. Displaying the true mark of loyal rooters,
they often identified their prize by the number he
wore. "There goes 88," said one little boy in an
excited whisper as Aaron Thomas worked his way
through the crowd. "I got 75," said another with
pride, waving the signature of Jim Katcavage.

To the autograph seekers, the players were
heroes all. And never did the Giants look so big as
when they bent to sign their names.

I particularly remember this scene because it
obviously made a deep impression on three-year-
old Angela. Later, as we waited for Fran to join us
in the campus dining hall, Angela noticed a
woman of imposing bearing in a white uniform
across the room. "Mommy," said Angela, "can I
have some paper? I want to get that lady's auto-
grass." I had no trouble explaining that the word
was autograph, but making clear why and from
whom they might be sought proved more difficult.

When Daddy is a professional athlete, some
unique problems can result. There are, I suspect,
few tots who can resist the temptation to preen in
the reflected glory of their father's prowess. Publicity, while helpful to an athlete—particularly in
the early stages of his career—can do serious
harm to a child's perspective of herself and to her
relationships with others. To guard against this,
we decided that whatever the needs and oppor-
tunities for Fran to make public appearances, his
family would not. I have tried to teach Angela
that her Daddy's job is no better and no worse, no

more important or less significant, than that of a doctor or a teacher, a salesman or a farmer. Sometimes Angela joins me in watching the Giants on television. The choice is hers, and with an interest span typical of her age, more often than not she soon forsakes football for a romp with the dog or the ritual bathing of a doll. One thing I do know; Angela will not follow in the footsteps of her father's career.

One further aspect of that career, and of pro football, that we should examine is the judgment of the officials and the penalties they exact.

Penalties (*sob*)

You watch your team's quarterback throw a 50-yard bomb for a touchdown. The stadium explodes with exultant cheers—that disintegrate into moans of disappointment. The reason? A yellow flag lies on the grass behind the quarterback, indicating that an official has detected a violation. And that means a penalty is in the offing.

A penalty is punishment for an infraction of the rules under which pro football is played. The seriousness of the infraction is reflected in the number of yards marked off against a team for each such infraction. The sight of the yellow marker on the grass, the announcer's voice mournfully reporting "There's a flag on the play"—both strike the distress of uncertainty in a fan's heart. Of course, there is always the chance that the penalty will be against the opposition. If it is, your team will have the opportunity to *accept* or *refuse* the penalty which is to be imposed—because football is a game of reasoned violence.

For example, in the situation above the flag might signal a foul by one of the defensive linemen who, in his zeal to chastise the QB, knocked him down well after the pass was already on its way.*

In that case, the offensive team will decline (refuse) the penalty since its acceptance would void the touchdown. Now, suppose the same circumstances prevail but the receiver drops the ball. The offensive team will accept the penalty, and the action will not be considered just an incomplete pass: The ball will be moved fifteen yards forward (from the line of scrimmage in the direction the offensive team is moving) and an automatic first down awarded.

However, suppose the flag near the QB signifies that one of the officials saw the fullback moving forward before the ball was snapped—incurring a *backfield illegally in motion* penalty of five yards. (No offensive player can move forward until the ball is snapped.) In that case, assuming our exemplary pass play went for a touchdown, the defense will accept the penalty; the ball is brought back (the touchdown is erased from the scoreboard, if not from the minds of fans and players) and 5 yards are marked off against the offense. The offense now gets to play the preceding down all over again—though this time, as a result of the penalty, it has to move the ball an extra 5 yards for a first down. Thus, if the touchdown pass was thrown on second and 7 (second down, 7 yards to go) the down will be replayed as second and 12—*still*

---

*This violation constitutes *roughing the passer*. For obvious reasons, I consider it to be the most heinous of gridiron crimes.

second down, but now 12 yards to go for a first down.

One last variation on this theme. Suppose that oft-referred-to pass was incomplete, the backfield was illegally in motion, and the action occurred on *third* down. The defense now has an interesting choice. If it accepts the penalty the offense is penalized 5 yards. If it declines the penalty, the offense is not penalized but doesn't get to replay the down. So, assuming that field position is such that the expected punt on fourth down will be forthcoming, the defense will probably decline the penalty.

The reasoning here is that it is always better to force a team to give up the ball (by confronting it with a punting situation, for example) than to accept a penalty which gives it another chance to score. (As you can see, on the football field it is better to receive than to give.) Like so many of football's seemingly inviolable principles, this one is occasionally broken.* But as a guideline it will serve the beginning fan well.

The significance of a penalty is that it can dramatically alter a game situation, as indicated

---

*One example: If a team is punting on fourth down from deep in its own territory and one of the offensive linemen is guilty of moving before the snap, the receiving (defensive) team may elect to accept the penalty if the punt is a long one and the punt return is minimal. The reasoning here is that the offense won't dare to try for a first down so close to its own goal (it didn't on the previous play, and it is now five yards worse off than before) and the punter may not kick as well and even if he does, there's the chance of a better punt return by the punt receiver.

by the earlier examples of the touchdown pass. Of course, not all penalties are equally important, but all do affect the game by improving or worsening a team's field position and permitting or denying possession.

According to the National and American Football Leagues' Digest of Rules, there are twenty-two rule infractions punishable by penalties of 5 yards, and fourteen infractions which earn 15-yard penalties. Only a super fan with a computerlike mind is familiar with all of them. But you should understand those which occur with some frequency. Here are some common 5-yard penalties:

Five-Yard Penalties

Understanding the terms *encroachment* and *offside* depends upon understanding the line of scrimmage. Earlier, for the sake of simplicity, the line of scrimmage was described as being where the ball is placed on the field. This is almost accurate—but not quite. There are really two lines of scrimmage separated by a *neutral zone*. When the ball is placed down on the field, the neutral zone is the area occupied by the length of the football and extended, in one's imagination, from sideline to sideline. Now, think of an imaginary line passing through both ends of the football, sideline to sideline. (These imaginary lines are really the boundaries of the neutral zone.) The through-the-nose line closest to the offensive team is its line of scrimmage; the through-the-nose line closest to the defense is its line of scrimmage.

ENCROACHMENT occurs when one of the linemen intrudes upon the neutral zone with any part of his body. The offensive center is exempt from this rule, since in positioning himself over the ball before the snap, his hands do encroach upon the forbidden area.

OFFSIDE occurs when a member of either team mistakenly invades the domain of his opponent. That is, he moves beyond his end of the football into the neutral zone or beyond it before the ball is snapped. If the malefactor is detected in this zone when the ball is snapped, he places his team in jeopardy of being penalized 5 yards—for offside. Notice, though, that there is no penalty if a player does not actually touch his opponent and is able to scramble back to his own side of the neutral zone before the ball is snapped.

KICKOFF OUT OF BOUNDS BETWEEN GOAL LINES WITHOUT BEING TOUCHED BY A PLAYER. It is perfectly permissible to kick the ball across the end line (10 yards beyond the goal line) on the kickoff, thus frustrating any return. The receiving team will then put the ball in play on its own 20-yard line. But if the ball goes out of bounds—before reaching the goal line—without being touched, the kicking team must rekick from 5 yards farther back from the original kickoff point.

FORWARD PASS BEYOND THE LINE OF SCRIMMAGE. Suppose the harried QB, under threat of being tackled, crosses his own line of scrimmage and throws a forward pass. He is immediately penalized 5 yards from the spot of the illegal pass, *plus loss of the down.* Example: Suppose our luckless QB is trying to pass on second and 8 from the 20-yard line. Defensive pressure forces him out of the pocket, and he begins to run with the ball. Then he decides to pass—although he has unknowingly crossed the line of scrimmage and is actually passing from the 21. Since his forward progress with the ball to the 21 was legal, he will be penalized 5 yards from the 21. Thus, the next play his team runs will be third down from the 16-yard line.

INVALID FAIR-CATCH SIGNAL. Sometimes when a ball is punted the kicking team covers* the receivers so swiftly that to attempt to return the punt would be suicide. In such cases, the punt receiver, seeing the kicking team bearing down on him, will raise his arm straight over his head. This signifies that in exchange for being allowed to catch the ball unmolested, he will not run with it after he makes the catch. Sometimes, though, the punt receiver is uncertain as to whether he should or shouldn't signal for a fair catch. He may uncertainly start to raise his arm and then drop it. Because the kicking team is penalized if it tackles the receiver after he has signaled for a fair catch, the fair-catch signal must be explicit. However, the receiver does not *have* to catch the ball. For example, if a receiver signals for a fair catch on his 10 he may elect not to catch the ball, hoping instead that it will roll into the end zone—resulting in a touchback, and placement of the ball on the 20.

DEFENSIVE HOLDING. This infraction is punishable by 5 yards and, in addition, the offense is awarded an automatic first down. Example: A tight end who is attempting to move downfield in order to catch a pass is prevented from getting

---

*"Covering" a punt means the kicking team blankets the punt receivers, allowing no significant return.

past the defensive LE by being held—literally—by the DLE's hands. Sportscasters often refer to this as "illegal use of hands on defense"—a grandiose but explicit description.

EXCEEDING THIRTY-SECOND PERIOD. This is the maximum time permitted an offensive team to agree on a play and initiate it.

FALSE START. A movement by an offensive player—generally a lineman—after he assumes a set position which creates the false impression that the snap has been made. This slight movement often results in a more obvious movement by his opponent—at least to the fans. Happily, virtue triumphs and the officials penalize only the offensive player.

ILLEGAL FORMATION. Applicable only to the offense and incurred by having less than seven players on the line of scrimmage. The split end is often the culprit when he inadvertently lines up in a backfield position. Thus the team fails to fulfill the seven-men-on-the-line requirement.

Other fairly common 5-yard penalties are *backfield in motion*, caused by having a back prematurely move forward at the snap, and *illegal procedure*, the result of premature movement by a lineman.

Fifteen-Yard Penalties

As you might expect, 15-yard penalties are for more serious and, in some cases, more dangerous infractions. Here are a few.*

* Many of these several penalties are imposed for *personal fouls*. This is a generic term for violations committed against the well-being of an individual

RUNNING INTO THE KICKER. This penalty, like several others in pro football, is designed to protect a player from injury by penalizing an excessive amount of violence. When a kicker is in the act of punting he is subject to a defensive rush similar to the pass rush against a quarterback. But the physical position of the kicker renders him particularly liable to injury. Like a ballet dancer, he will have one foot high in the air as the kicking leg follows through, the weight of the body supported on the toes of the other leg. Obviously, he is in no position to take evasive action. This rule does offer some protection. It provides that no player may touch the kicker in an attempt to block a punt *unless* the player simultaneously at least touches the ball—along with the kicker's leg. For running into the kicker "gently," the penalty is 5 yards and an automatic first down. But for crashing into the kicker—without blocking the kick—the penalty is 15 yards and an automatic first down. Since punting is a result of failure to move the ball to a first down, punters who experience even the mildest rush often act as though they have been grievously wounded. Arms flailing, they crumple to the ground with cries of pain. The officials, however, are rarely fooled. Notice that the choice—a penalty of 5 yards, or of 15 yards—is left to the discretion of the officials. It is a judgment call.

FAIR-CATCH INTERFERENCE is usually the result of some zealous lineman who, in his haste to get

---

player, as opposed to noncontact infractions of the rules. Personal fouls include such actions as striking with the fists, kicking, kneeing, running into or roughing the kicker, roughing the passer, and other displays of physical exuberance.

downfield under a punt and contain the receiver, doesn't see the fair-catch sign and goes crashing into him. Penalty: 15 yards for overzealousness.

CLIPPING is one of the most common 15 yarders. A *clip* is a block delivered from behind a player, or from the rear. It is illegal everywhere except in close line play—an area 3 yards on either side of the line of scrimmage extending laterally to the position ordinarily occupied by the *defensive* tackles.

GRABBING THE FACE MASK seems to occur about once a game. The face mask—the protective wire grid across the front of a helmet—is an appealing handle begging to be grasped. But to surrender to the impulse costs "15 big ones," as the sports-casters say.

OFFENSIVE HOLDING is generally a result of a defender being just about to slip by an offensive lineman and the latter surrendering to human nature and grabbing him with his hand. The offensive linemen can block in a variety of ways but, as you already know, they may not use their hands.

PILING ON is called when a player has been tackled, the whistle blows—signaling that the ball is dead—and another defender flies through the air and crumps into the prostrate ball carrier or pass receiver. It is usually just a matter of overexuberance, but there is a marvelous folklore of feuds waged between various offensive and defensive players in which piling on figures dramatically. Needless to say, the folklore is ancient history, and in today's professional ball no such muscular hanky-panky is tolerated, at least not if you get caught. Another penalty for aggravated violence is for UNNECESSARY ROUGHNESS, which is self-explanatory.

When a pass is thrown, both receiver and defender have an equal right to go for the ball—one seeking the reception, the other an interception. OFFENSIVE PASS INTERFERENCE results from a receiver interfering with the freedom of action of a defensive halfback. DEFENSIVE PASS INTERFERENCE is the converse, and gives the offense an automatic first down from the point of the foul.

INTENTIONALLY GROUNDING A PASS. Sometimes even the most courageous QB finds his receivers are covered, the defensive linemen closing in about him. One strategem for escaping from this situation is to throw the ball out of bounds—but within "legitimate" proximity to a receiver. However, if in an official's judgment the action of the passer was a deliberate attempt to avoid a loss of yardage —as a result of being tackled—by throwing the ball away, the penalty is heavy: 15 yards *and* loss of down.

Two other penalty situations are also encountered with some frequency. If team A throws a pass into the opponent's end zone and a defender interferes with a receiver, the ball is given to the offense on the 1-yard line of their opponent. *No touchdown can be scored as a result of a penalty.*

The next situation is traditionally a difficult one for most fans to grasp, so I shall resort to quoting the rule book: "If a distance penalty, enforced from a specified spot between the goal lines, would carry the ball more than half the distance to offender's goal line, penalty shall be half the distance from that spot to their goal line."

Suppose your team has the ball on its own 30-

yard line and is found guilty of (offensive) holding. The ball will be moved back to the 15. But suppose the same infraction occurs on the 25. The ball is then moved to a distance of 12½ yards from the goal line. This is what the sportscaster means when he refers to being "penalized half the distance to the goal line."

The Official's Life

The life of a pro-football official is almost as trying as that of a player. Like the players, the officials must go all out on every play; never relax their scrutiny of every phase of the game, regardless of how one-sided the score may be; be physically able to keep up with the game—for example, they must be prepared to cover swift receivers and defenders as play patterns develop. And always, they must be in position to ensure the legality of play everywhere on the field—an exhausting responsibility. Nor is their life entirely free from on-the-field violence, despite their noncombative status. A runner breaking through the line sometimes zigs past an official who is then zagged by an anxious linebacker. And when a pass receiver is tackled, not infrequently the rolling bodies bring down the official whose on-the-spot presence is required.

One incipient danger is that a player whose team is being penalized for an infraction he committed simply loses his temper. At such times the player may stamp his feet, invoke heaven as witness to his innocence, or move threateningly toward the official who made the call—looking very large and very hostile. Disparagement of an offi-

cial—let alone pushing or hitting one—is sum-
mary cause for severe disciplinary action. (However, officials tend to tolerate imprecations uttered
during the heat of battle.) You will notice that
whenever a brouhaha about an official's call
seems imminent, the outraged player (or players)
will be soothed by teammates and led away—
from the danger of eviction from the game.

Sometimes fights erupt on the field between
opposing players. Here again, intervention—if not
pacification—by their teammates will be swift.
Football fights usually look more damaging than
they are. The players are fairly well protected from
injury—at least from swinging fists. There's a story
that sheds some light on this that is told about
Jack Stroud, formerly an offensive lineman with
the Giants. Mr. Stroud was a formidable man,
widely reputed to be the strongest man in pro
football. One day a fight started between the
Giants, then on defense, and their opponents.
Both benches quickly emptied as the players, including Stroud, ran up to join the fracas. One of
the coaches, to his surprise, noted Stroud running
back to the bench, while the fight continued un-
abated. Said Stroud, with a wry grin, "I forgot my
helmet."

Although most players would die before admit-
ting so publicly, they privately agree that the
officials do a fine job—most of the time. The fans,
whatever their private opinions, publicly boo the
officials either matter of factly or with feeling,
depending on the game situation. But then no fan
lists dispassionate appraisal on the inventory of
feelings he brings to a game.

When television introduced the isolated camera/instant-replay technique, some fans thought that the ability to take another look at the action— even in slow motion—would reveal many inaccuracies in officiating. That this has not happened is certainly a tribute to pro football's keen-eyed officials.

Television may not have revolutionized the officials, but it has created a new breed of fan— one whose Sunday afternoon perch is increasingly, not the stadium seat, but the armchair.

The Armchair Fan

Pro football isn't available for rerun watching during the summer, and the game's heroes (and villains) can change faster than you can say "recovered fumble" or "touchdown." The fascination of pro football is its unpredictability—the awesome or awful promise to be realized as each play unfolds. It is not a game that can be summarized by a box score. It must be watched—observed as it happens, whether on television or from a seat in the stands. Even if you do occasionally (or always) go to the stadium to watch your team play at home, you will certainly be part of the television audience for their games on the road. So here is some advice—culled from friends as well as from personal experience—which may be helpful to armchair fans.

Every wife is familiar with any man's peculiar chronology of eating. Let a television program she's watching approach its climax or the mystery she is reading be poised to reveal who the real criminal is, and, with clockwork dependability, hubby will declare he is starving. Dutiful wife that she is, the denouement on TV passes unseen and identification of the criminal is postponed until later. With the kickoff scheduled at 1:00 or 1:30 P.M., and a televised pre-game show beginning a half hour or an hour earlier, your first act of pro-football fandom is to escape from incarceration in the kitchen.

One solution is to make sandwiches before the game and keep them ready to respond to plaintive cries of hunger. Another is to pack a tray with an assortment of cold cuts and breads and set up a smörgasbord table—complete with ice, glasses, beverages, or whatever—in the TV room. This technique has the twin virtues of providing your starving companion with victuals—and of tacitly making clear that he can help himself. Even so, if you make yourself a sandwich you can expect to hear the familiar, "As long as you're up . . ."

I know one family in pro football who has season tickets to its team's home games and, when the team is playing away, simulates stadium attendance. Early in the week the wife makes up a roster of the opposition, listing each player by name, number, the position he plays, his height and weight. A quantity of similar rosters long since has been prepared for the home team—all courtesy of hubby's office copying machine. Friends and neighbors are invited over for the pre-game show and the rosters are distributed—along with pennants in support of their traveling heroes—and the group settles back to an afternoon of football. To provide sustenance for the assembled rooters, each wife is made a "vendor"—responsible for hot dogs (kept warm in the kitchen), soft drinks, peanuts, et al. On one occasion, though, a note of discord was struck by a couple who had only recently moved into the neighborhood from a distant city. They brought their own pennants along —supporting the team playing against the one favored by their hosts. Fortunately for the delicate balance of neighborhood relations, the game ended in a 14–14 tie.

There are some special advantages to watching—and listening—to pro football on television. The zoom lens of the camera gives the viewer an intimacy with the QB that is impossible to duplicate by any other means—even by attending a game in person. Conversely, the limitation of televised pro ball is that you do not get the panoramic feeling of an entire eleven-man offensive formation confronting an eleven-man defensive unit. This small deficiency is of concern only to a minority of postgraduate fans. It takes great discipline—certainly more than I have—to take your eyes off the QB and survey the entire football scene. In any case, television's isolated camera and video-tape replay give you a unique opportunity to see what the other players were doing while you were watching the ball.

For example, the camera—live—will stay glued to the quarterback as he drops back, coolly ignores the defensive rush, and passes. You, and the camera, will follow the flight of the ball until suddenly and almost inexplicably the split end appears on camera and makes the reception. The "other half" of this play is, of course, how the receiver ran his pattern, eluded the covering defender, and made the catch. And that is what the video-tape/isolated-camera view will reveal.

You will see the split end down in his three-point stance, watch him move downfield, fake to the inside, then cut toward the sideline and make the catch just before the defender bounces him out of bounds. The camera will also show you an official holding both arms out—as though cradling a baby—to indicate that the completion was made in bounds. (Sideline catches are occasionally a matter of some dispute. If the pass is to be legally completed, the receiver must have both feet in bounds—that is, on the playing surface.)

Television's instant replay should also get a measure of credit for the fans' growing appreciation of the importance of the defense. On a running play, for example, the live-action camera sequence will follow the QB's hand-off to a back, and the runner's progress around or through the line. The video-tape replay will show the action on the other side of the line: the linebacker warily appraising the offense and sensing—through experience and instinct—where the play will develop, fighting off a block, and coming up to make the tackle.

A satisfying emotional feature of watching instant replay is that you can savor again your team's heroics—the long touchdown pass, the long run from scrimmage, the inspirational kickoff return for a touchdown. Alas, the tape also recapitulates moments of despair—the tragedies of interceptions and fumbles, of uncovered receivers and missed tackles.

Half time—the interval between the end of the

second and beginning of the third quarters—is a twenty-minute break of convenience. You can check on where the kids are and what mischief they've committed, load up the dishwasher, replenish the snack tray, and empty the ashtrays. Or better still, you can watch the half-time show. Its colorful pageantry is unique to football.

If you live within that area in which televised coverage of a team's home game is blacked out, you can wangle an invitation to the home of a suburban friend who can get the game on TV. Or you might organize a party to be held in a suburban motel which receives televised coverage. In such cases, of course, everyone shares in the rental cost of the room—but make sure that the motel doesn't stipulate a maximum number of guests per room, an increasingly common practice since home games became regular sellouts and enterprising metropolitan fans descended upon suburban motels, cramming fifteen or more into a single room to lower the prorated cost per fan.

Radio coverage of home games is unaffected by the local TV blackout, and radio pays a special dividend. As I mentioned earlier, just because there is no accompanying picture for the description to lean on, the radio sportscaster will amplify details of the game action which might otherwise continue to mystify you. So if the game is not on TV, by all means give radio an ear.

Another virtue of pro football is that it gives you an opportunity to satisfy painlessly one of a wife's most boring tasks: ironing. Many women love to cook, and not a few derive some pleasure from keeping their homes free of dust. The washing machine has made tolerable the tedium of doing the laundry—but I have yet to meet a woman who felt anything other than hostility towards ironing (ugh). Ironing to the accompaniment of pro football can help you accomplish this burdensome, time-consuming chore almost before you realize it. But have care.

I remember one Sunday afternoon when I was crouched over my ironing board watching the Giants play an exhibition game against the Green Bay Packers. (Exhibition game or not, every team wants to win—and that's especially true against the Packers, who dominated pro football for many years. Moreover, the Packers had administered a series of drubbings to the Giants the last few times they had met.) There were only a couple of minutes left in the game and although we trailed, the game was still close and a touchdown would give us victory. With the seconds ticking away, the Giants moved down the field. The crowd in Lambeau Field roared encouragement to the Packers, while I implored Fran and the Giants onward. A series of sideline passes carried us smartly down the field until we penetrated inside the Packer 20. There, the Green Bay defense stiffened and three downs were consumed without appreciable success. It was fourth down now. The crowd in the stands was momentarily still, but with exultant cheers held ready in their throats for the moment when the great Packer defense would hold the Giants and Green Bay would take over the ball. You could feel the tension, the conflicting thrust of irresistible force and immovable object.

I was transfixed, my mind filled with the absolute this-is-it sense of finality that is the emotional peak of every pro-football game. Fran took the snap, rolled left, spotted Joe Morrison in the end zone, and threw.

Touchdown!

It was a moment of sweet success for my husband's team and I enjoyed it too, if vicariously. The success didn't smell sweet, though, more like something burning. It was—Fran's favorite sport shirt.*

Of course, one way to watch pro football and stay free from the hazards of ironing is to go to the game.

*I would be happy to accept a one-to-one ratio of burned shirts to touchdown passes. Unhappily, I think my wife enjoys a long lead over me.

The Stadium Fan

You're one of the lucky ones. Your husband has tickets for today's game and he's invited you—grudgingly or otherwise—to go with him. Now you're going to participate in what has become a Sunday afternoon American ritual. Indeed, pro football has become so popular that a number of fans have attempted to include the disposition of their season tickets in their last will and testament. (They were prevented from making such bequests by a League rule which prohibits the transfer of season tickets other than by the ticket offices of the various teams.)

Probably the first thing you will think about is what to wear—after all, you're a woman first and a football fan second. And your concern with clothes is well founded. Though the motto of today's generation of swingers may be "keep cool," your primary concern will be how to keep warm.

Autumn afternoons can be deceptive. Their warm promise often remains chillingly unfulfilled. Moreover, regardless of whether your stadium seats are located under the protective overhang of another deck or the roof, you can usually depend on the temperature being colder than you anticipate. (Note to fans in Los Angeles, Miami, New Orleans, and Atlanta: This weather warning is, of course, less significant if you live in milder climes.)

Unless you want to earn an instant reputation for exotica, dress sensibly. Don't disregard the dictates of fashion entirely—heaven forbid!—but do select what you will wear with an eye to practical comfort. And that means making sure your husband is going to be comfortable with you along, too.

Even though more and more women are going to pro-football games, there is a distinctly male aura about the game. It's rather as though a gentleman's private club which forbade women to go beyond the lobby now allowed them the run of the place. Despite the change in rules, some of the old members haven't quite adjusted to the idea. Similarly, there is a hard corps of veteran pro-football fans who know you have every right to be in the stadium but still can't understand what you're doing there.

So, for these reasons and others, wear slacks. Or a pants suit. Or a skirt with opaque panty hose. Wear low heels—it can be quite a hike from the parking lot to your seat, and the stairs on each deck that give access to the seats range from steep to practically perpendicular, surely no place to totter about on high heels.

Even before you get to the stadium you may encounter a social phenomenon that has accompanied the meteoric rise of fan interest in pro football: tailgating.

Many couples go to pro-football games in foursomes, often in the same station wagon. They arrive at the stadium parking lot well before game time and settle down for lunch. And not just cold sandwiches, either.

Part of the tailgating ritual seems to depend upon a small charcoal grill—a Japanese hibachi, for example—on which hamburgers and hot dogs, shishkebab or stew are prepared. The grill, of course, is placed on the ground and the lowered tailgate becomes a table. You can make the cuisine and ambiance as simple or as sophisticated as you wish.

I remember pulling into the parking area reserved for players behind Yankee Stadium and observing the ultimate in tailgating. The wife— and still a good friend—of one of the Giants was holding court in the shadow of a sparkling new Dodge wagon. Together with some of her friends, they formed a semicircle around the tailgate of the Dodge, which was hidden by a damask table cloth. A candle in a silver holder sputtered in the gentle breeze.

A magnum of red wine leaned negligently against a tire, and the unmistakable aroma of beef Stroganoff was in the air. That it was something of a put-on was confirmed by the paper cups in lieu of wine glasses. But as you can see, tailgating doesn't condemn you to roughing it.

Bring a pair of binoculars with you. They give you an on-the-field intimacy not otherwise obtainable. Binoculars also help restore a human quality to the players. Remember, the men inside those uniforms are indeed human, and with binoculars you can see the expression on their faces—the disgust or delight, fatigue or enthusiasm.

A mini-radio—one of those all-transistor pocket-sized portables—is a great help for the beginning football fan. By listening to the radio description of the game you'll get a professional explanation—a word portrait of what is happening. You can also learn why a certain player isn't starting, or how serious is the injury that forced another player to leave the game.

Perhaps the radio's greatest contribution to your enjoyment is this: It will answer most, if not all, of the questions you would otherwise direct at your husband. And nothing, literally *nothing* will upset your devoted spouse more than having to explain what happened on the last play while the next one is already unfolding. Also, the radio sportscaster's expertise can become your own—particularly if you hold it close to your ear and keep the volume low.

For example, if a running play has gained good yardage the radio will probably whisper its appreciative commentary on the game. This enables you to remark to your companion that "the trap blocking was really crisp." Or, after a fine kickoff return, that the runner "made a great cut."

If at first you don't completely understand the subtle meanings of what you are parroting, don't worry, you soon will. And you are certain to reap a reward of grudging recognition among the male fans around you—perhaps even the ultimate, "She really knows her football." Meanwhile your husband will feel both proud and relieved.

About the time near the end of the first half

that the officials issue the two-minute warning, the band and accompanying cheerleaders ease themselves off the folding chairs they've been occupying in a corner of the stadium and, with an occasional warm-up thump and toot, prepare to march onto the field for the half-time festivities. The drums begin their urgent rhythm and the band marches onto the field with drill-team precision. Preceding them are one or more high-stepping drum majorettes, twirling batons with a dexterity that belies their nervousness. I know they are nervous, because I was the drum majorette at the University of Georgia, where, incidentally, I met my husband.*

In pro football, the half-time show is usually built around a celebrated college marching band (or occasionally a prize-winning high-school one) that not only plays special arrangements of popular music but simultaneously executes complicated marching routines. Without missing a beat, the ranks of the band move in opposite directions, then crisscross together in an intricate display of carefully rehearsed precision. The drums, the blaring horns, the hundred or more brightly uniformed figures with their plumed shakos, the sun glinting from the spinning batons of the drum

*It was popularly believed by most of the members of the University of Georgia football team on which I played that the drum majorettes only saw half of the football games we played—the second half. We thought, with some legitimacy, that the girls spent the first half in an agony of tension over their role in the half-time show, alternately chewing and filing their fingernails.

majorettes—all contribute to this exciting football panoply.

There is an old football saying, "The ball draws a crowd," meaning that the defenders will be drawn to it like flies to honey. Throughout the game, you will find it difficult to follow any action other than that which involves the ball—from the snap to the QB's hand-off or his pass. But do try, even though it takes great ocular discipline, to watch the other offensive players as they fulfill their individual assignments. And do try to focus on a single defensive player as he reacts to the upcoming play.

If you watch the offensive guards and see them pull, you will be among the first to know that a running play is about to develop. If you are following the pattern of a pass receiver, you'll be able to watch his continuing battle with the defender who is covering him.

He may make a spectacular catch of a pass. Or he may just run out his pattern—knowing, as you didn't, that a running play was called in the huddle.

There is a special fascination in watching the performance of each player. If you only follow the QB, you'll miss the desperate head-to-head battle between the offensive and defensive linemen—particularly on a pass play. You won't see the DE fake to the inside and then twist around the outside, fend off a block, and demolish the quarterback before he can throw.*

*I think you could have selected some other examples for defensive heroics. Why pick on the quarterback?

Every one of the twenty-two football players on the field is fighting a very personal battle with a very personal enemy. Each individual, silent struggle is an essential part of the whole—of a single play, a quarter, a game.

The Last Word

I have tried to give the reader not only a basic understanding of the how and why of professional football, but an insight into the game's enormous appeal—an appeal which holds millions of fans in rapt concentration from kickoff to final gun. Already, pro football's adherents include many women. They have discovered that it is not "his" game, but *ours*.

If this book is successful, there will now be one more pro-football fan in your house.

You.

Glossary

Professional football has its own special language, words and phrases which every fan must understand if she wants to talk fluently about her favorite game. As a matter of linguistic fact, it is often impossible to comprehend what is happening on the field if you aren't familiar with gridiron jargon—particularly if you listen to the game on radio. At first, you may have to consciously memorize parts of this vocabulary, but with increasing exposure to pro football—whether from the stands or via television or radio—the words will become familiar. You will understand what they mean, and other fans will understand you.

Aerial: A forward pass.
Attitude: Referring to a team's esprit de corps. Being "up for a game" is a function of good attitude.
Automatics: Numbers or words which, when the QB inserts them in his signal call, change the play. Also known as audibles, check signals, and, more

loquaciously, as "changing the call at the line of scrimmage."

Balance: Said of a player, usually a back, so sure on his feet that he is difficult to bring down.

Balanced line: Three linemen—a guard, a tackle, an end—on both sides of the center.

Blitz: Originally a reference to a defensive back— usually the weak-side safety—who leaves his normal defensive position and attempts to break through the line to reach the QB. The term is often applied (if you're a purist, misapplied) to the same action by linebackers. See *Red dog.*

Bomb: A very long pass to a receiver going deep.

Bootleg: Describes the act of a QB running in opposite direction from the apparent movement of the play, while hiding the ball on his hip.

Cutback: The sharp change of direction of a ball carrier heading to the outside and suddenly veering to the inside.

Double-team: Two offensive linemen blocking one defender; or two defenders guarding one receiver.

Forward progress: The point at which the ball carrier's progress toward the opponent's goal line is halted by the defenders. Barring penalties, it is the point at which the ball will be put in play on the next down. Note that regardless of how far back a carrier is shoved by gang-tackling defenders, only his forward progress—the yards or inches he gained—is recorded, and nothing is subtracted even if the defenders shove him back to the locker room. Of course, this assumes he made it across the line of scrimmage—that he achieved a measurable gain.

Flea flicker: Any wildly fanciful play of the kind usually seen in playgrounds but rare in professional football. The Giants have a famous one: a triple reverse with the QB getting the ball and passing for a touchdown. It actually worked (once) against Pittsburgh.

Flood area: When all or several eligible receivers run their patterns into a designated area of the opponent's territory. An offensive tactic frequently used against *zone* defense.

"I" formation: An offensive alignment in which at least three backs—including the QB—line up directly behind the center.

Keying: When a defender has responsibility for a particular offensive player and operates as his "shadow," moving with him (on opposite sides of the line of scrimmage, of course) wherever he goes.

Man-for-man: Pass defense in which one defensive back is responsible for covering one receiver.

Mousetrap: See *Trap.*

Onside kick: A short rolling kick—one that is difficult for the up-front members of the receiving team to field cleanly. The kick following a touchdown or safety must travel a minimum of 10 yards. Thereafter it is anybody's ball and if recovered by the kicking team, theirs.

Option play: The ball carrier can either run or pass. Often specified as "halfback option," or "fullback option."

Pitchout: QB takes the center snap, pivots, and tosses underhand to a back who is usually in motion.

Plays loose: Of a defensive back who doesn't get too close to a fast receiver. The opposite of *Plays tight.*

Plays tight: Extremely close coverage of receivers

by the defensive secondary. If the defenders can stay with the receivers it will make a pass completion that much more difficult, but the more closely the defenders guard the receivers the greater the likelihood that a successful fake will enable the receiver to score a long gain.

Quarterback sneak: QB takes the snap from center and plunges directly ahead.

Quick opener: Short plunge through the line by a halfback without any faking (by the QB) before the hand-off is accomplished.

Red dog: The act of one or more linebackers crashing through the offensive line at the snap. Target: the quarterback. Red dog is sometimes shortened to *dog.* Other terms synonymous with red dog are *blitz,* which can also apply to a "red dog" by the weak-side linebacker; shooting, and storming.

Run to daylight: Former coach Vince Lombardi of the Green Bay Packers made this football imperative a household word. Strictly speaking, it means that if a ball carrier on a running play finds the hole blocked, he should innovate and look elsewhere for an opening in the line; also refers to a ball carrier's singular mission in life: to drive, drive, drive for a touchdown.

Second effort: The refusal of a ball carrier to submit to the first attempt to halt his progress and thereby gain additional yardage.

Slotback: Halfback who lines up directly behind the hole created by the end splitting. From this position he is essentially a receiver.

Taxi squad: Includes those players who, although under contract to a team and allowed to participate in its practice sessions, are not on the official roster and therefore cannot play in League games. When a regular player is injured, his replacement is usually a player promoted from the taxi squad.

Trap: When an offensive interior lineman—most often a guard—pulls out of line and blocks a defensive tackle or end who has been "allowed" to come through the line.

Two on one: Two offensive players blocking one defensive player. Also see *Double-teaming.*

Zone defense: A pass defense in which each member of the secondary, as well as the linebackers, is personally responsible for a designated area of the playing field. As a receiver moves from one such designated area to another, the defender will "pass" his covering responsibility to the defender responsible for the area the receiver is entering.

Appendix: Formations

There are two basic football formations—the "T" and the single wing. The latter is something of an anachronism, at least in pro football, and as such is of only academic interest to us.

All pro-football formations are variations of the "T." Since there are practically limitless ways to vary an offensive formation—by using men in motion; flankers; "weighting" one side of the formation with all or most receivers, for example—the fledgling fan can hardly be expected to recognize all the variations as they appear in a game. But some are especially common, or intriguing, and you can, after only brief hesitation, learn to spot these.

In the diagrams that follow, X marks the spot of the offensive center.

The Tight "T"

This is the classic pro-football formation, now used mostly in short yardage situations. The offensive line is balanced. The left end is not split, and there are two halfbacks and no flanker. The quarterback is directly behind the center, the fullback immediately behind the quarterback. The halfbacks are generally aligned with (or inside of) the tackles and flank the fullback. The name of the formation springs from the position of the four backs and the center, forming a "T." In a "Split T" there are gaps of varying size between the linemen —as a consequence of which the defense is spread apart, thereby giving the offensive linemen better block angles.

Strong Right

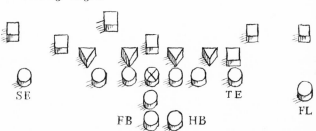

In this formation one of the halfbacks has become a flanker. The remaining HB is to the same side— in this case, the right side—as the flanker.

Triple Right

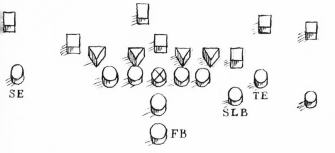

Only the fullback is behind the quarterback. One halfback has become a flankerback, the other a slotback. Thus the quarterback has three receivers on the right side—slotback; flanker; tight end— and one receiver to the left, the split end.

Double Wing

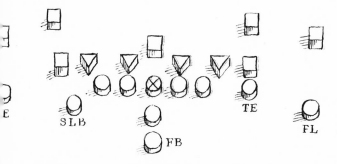

Here again, the only backfield protection the quarterback has is provided by the fullback. But the slotback is to the left, creating two "wings" of receivers.

Shotgun

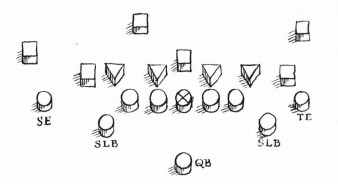

The quarterback is now stripped of backfield pass blocking. But he has five receivers available to run their patterns. Notice that the quarterback is positioned several yards behind the center. In effect, the time he has to pass is decreased by the absence of backfield blocking, but somewhat increased by his extreme distance from the line of scrimmage. The asset of the shotgun is that five receivers put an enormous strain on the defensive coverage; the weakness, that the quarterback is, in terms of pass protection, almost naked. In general, a team will not break its huddle and immediately assume this formation, but camouflage its intentions by shifting into the shotgun from a more standard formation. This is calculated to surprise the defense and limit its ability to adjust to the passing firepower of the shotgun.